Our Royal Baby

Scholastic Children's Books,
Euston House, 24 Eversholt Street,
London NW1 1DB, UK

A division of Scholastic Ltd
London ~ New York ~ Toronto ~ Sydney ~ Auckland
Mexico City ~ New Delhi ~ Hong Kong

Editor: Elizabeth Scoggins

Published in the UK by Scholastic Ltd, 2013

Written by Sue McMillan
© Scholastic Children's Books, 2013

ISBN 978 1407 13861 9

Printed and bound by Bell & Bain Ltd, United Kingdom

2 4 6 8 10 9 7 5 3 1

Papers used by Scholastic Children's Books are made from woods grown in
sustainable forests.

Our Royal Baby

Sue McMillan

SCHOLASTIC

Contents

And Baby Makes Three

Since their first days together at university, the Duke and Duchess of Cambridge have wowed the world with their thoroughly modern romance.

Once the confetti was swept away after their magical wedding day, the eager anticipation of the pitter-patter of tiny (royal) feet began.

At long last, that moment is here and we can welcome the latest and very special addition to the royal family, as baby makes three…

Every baby is special to their mum and dad – the apple of their eye and the centre of their world. But the new royal arrival has a very big pair of bootees to fill as third in line to the British throne after grandfather, Prince Charles and father, William.

Yet all three may have long wait, as William's grandmother, the Queen, shows no signs of slowing down too much yet, even at the ripe old age of 87!

Did you know?

Before 2012, if William and Kate had had a baby girl followed by a boy, the son would have been William's heir to the throne, even though he was younger. A law change means that from now on, the eldest child is heir, whether it is a boy or girl.

Their official title may be the Duke and Duchess of Cambridge, but they are affectionately called William and Kate by royal-watchers.

The Duke and Duchess are two of the most photographed people in the world, whether they are attending glamorous parties, doing charity work or just relaxing. Whatever the occasion though, one thing is always on show – their love for one another.

The loved-up couple's life will go through many changes with the new arrival. Their quiet cottage in Anglesey, and their home at Nottingham Cottage, below, will be given up for a family home. It is thought the royal couple will plump for apartment 1a in Kensington Palace, which once belonged to Princess Margaret, who was the Queen's sister. The couple are also keen to have a country home to retreat to, and it is rumoured that

Anmer Hall on the Queen's Sandringham estate in Norfolk is their preferred spot.

A place to relax will be important for the couple as they ease into life as full-time royals. William has grown up as a royal, and although Kate has proved a natural in her new role, the new family will need time away from public life to share precious time with their new little one.

A Young Prince

Thirty-one years ago, the world went gaga over another royal arrival, as we celebrated the birth of Prince William. Or, to give him his full name – William Arthur Phillip Louis Windsor!

Fact File

Born …   21:03 BST on 21st June 1982
At …   St Mary's Hospital, London
Weight …   3.4kg (7lbs 5oz)
Star sign …   Cancer
Royal status … second in line to the throne
Trivia …   the first royal born in hospital

William is the elder son of Prince Charles and his first wife, Diana, Princess of Wales. The pair first met when Lady Diana Spencer was a shy 19 year-old nanny. After a brief romance they married in 1981 at St Paul's Cathedral, in a lavish, fairytale wedding watched by 750 million people worldwide. The birth of William just a year later was the icing on the royal cake, with his younger brother, Harry, arriving in 1984.

As a lively and sometimes cheeky young boy William was nicknamed 'Your royal naughtiness' by Diana. He had several nannies, but Charles and Diana were more involved in their children's upbringing than previous generations and Diana was often pictured on trips out with her boys. Naturally, William and Kate also want to be hands on, so they have not employed a nanny, which means our future king may be doing the night-time nappy-changes!

Traditionally, royal children had been taught at home by a tutor until the age of eight. Charles and Diana decided to do things differently, so William racked up another first when he went to nursery at Mrs Mynor's School in London.

Stints at two prep schools followed, and at 13, William went to Eton, one of Britain's top public schools. It is just across the River Thames from Windsor Castle, one of the royal residences, so William often visited his granny, the Queen, for tea.

Her support helped William deal with the pain of his parents' divorce and the heartbreak of his mother Diana's death in a car accident in 1997.

Diana's death made her sons closer and although William is more serious than Harry, the pair are the best of friends. They also have a close and relaxed relationship with their father, Prince Charles.

As well as spending time swishing down the ski slopes at Klosters, William also played sport at Eton, including soccer and his favourite, water polo. He also took part in the 'field game' a mix of football and rugby created by the school.

At 18, William left school and had a gap year. He spent time in Africa and Belize, and went to Chile to work with children through the charity Raleigh International.

On his return, William began a degree in history of art at the University St Andrews in Scotland. Not surprisingly, there were record numbers of applications that year, with many girls dreaming they would catch the eye of the dashing young prince and become a princess one day!

Halfway through his degree, William decided to swap his main subject to Geography and, in 2005, he graduated with an upper second degree, the best result for a royal at university.

Did you know?

Since he was a young boy, William's parents had encouraged him to get involved with charities. In 2004, William was so moved when he saw the destruction caused by the Boxing Day tsunami in the Indian Ocean that he volunteered at a Red Cross warehouse with his brother, Harry, packing supplies for survivors.

As he has grown older, William has taken on more royal duties and works for many good causes. He still supports some of Diana's favourite charities and now regularly visits patients at the Royal Marsden hospital in London.

William has certainly inherited his mother's warmth and ability for making people feel at ease. Even so, it must be a bit of a surprise for patients to see the future king standing with his sleeves rolled up, offering them a cup of tea!

In 2009, William and Harry set up a foundation to support charities working with causes close to their hearts – helping young people, members of the armed forces, and conservation projects. When William married Kate, she joined their foundation and it was renamed the *Royal Foundation of the Duke and Duchess of Cambridge and Prince Harry*.

An Ordinary Girl

When Catherine Elizabeth Middleton made her entrance into the world in January 1982, no one could have guessed that she would one day be the wife of the future king.

Fact File

Born ... on 9th January 1982
At ... The Royal Berkshire Hospital
Star sign ... Capricorn
Siblings ... Philippa (Pippa) and James
Trivia ... Kate lived in Amman, Jordan as a small child

Kate's early life was a world away from William's royal upbringing. When she was small, her parents, Carole and Michael, both worked for British Airways. Carole was a flight attendant and Michael was a flight dispatcher – helping planes take off safely.

After Kate, Pippa and James were born, Carole decided to start up a mail-order business selling party items, which is run from their home in Bucklebury, Berkshire.

The Middleton family is very close and Kate always turns to them for support. Before her engagement to William she was often pictured out and about with her younger sister, Pippa, who is also one of her closest friends.

Kate is also close to her brother and parents and spends time with them whenever she can. William and Kate even spent Christmas Day in Bucklebury and William is said to enjoy relaxing in their welcoming home, away from public life.

Although Kate's family is far more ordinary than William's, she had a comfortable, happy childhood. In 1989, Kate started at St Andrew's School in Pangbourne, Berkshire. Outside school, she was a member of her local Brownie pack and often went camping and on trips with them.

At the age of 13, Kate moved to Downe House for two terms, but found it hard to settle in the all girls school.

A move to a mixed school, Marlborough College, followed and Kate was much happier there. She was known for being a quiet, bright girl who was athletic and also enjoyed acting.

It would have been easy for Kate's classmates to have been jealous of her success, but she was popular at school and her classmates called her 'princess in waiting'. Who knew back then that they were predicting her future?

Did you know?

When people looked at Kate's family tree some amazing facts came out. Kate's grandfather on her mum's side was a working class coal miner. But going further back in history, it seems there was already a royal link – one of Kate's distant relatives was the niece of Henry VIII's second wife, Anne Boleyn!

Like William, Kate enjoys playing sports. At Marlborough College, she was captain of the school's hockey team and has recently shown that she hadn't lost any of her skills with a hockey stick.

She also played tennis and netball, and was very good at high jump, as well as being a star cross-country runner. So it's fair to say that Kate was an all-round school sports star and you can bet she was probably first-pick for any team.

Twice Kate and William's almost crossed paths before they first met. First, when William played a hockey match at her prep school then during Kate's gap year, when she took part in Raleigh International in Chile, just weeks after the Prince. During the rest of her year off, Kate spent time in Florence, and sailing on the Solent off the Isle of Wight. But it wouldn't be long before she did meet her handsome prince…

Like many students at Marlborough College, Kate decided to head north to university and picked St Andrews, a small Scottish university town on the east coast.

No one really knows if the rumour is true that she already had a crush on Prince William. Some friends claimed that she had a picture of him on her wall at school, which Kate laughed off in an interview saying, "No, I had the Levi's guy on my wall, not a picture of William."

One thing is for sure – applications to study there jumped when people heard William would be starting there in 2001. Many girls were desperate for the chance to bag a prince, or even just to say they had studied with him.

Kate, who was studying history of art with William, was different. She wasn't showy or loud and it was her quiet, natural manner that started their friendship.

A Royal Romance

Although they were on the same course and just rooms apart in their halls of residence, it was in the dining room that William first plucked up the courage to ask Kate to join him for breakfast after her early morning run.

Chatting over their muesli, the pair realized they had loads in common, from their love of the countryside, to swimming and skiing, not to mention their gap year experience in Chile!

At first, the pair were nothing more than friends. But a fashion show changed that.

It was during their second term that William fell for Kate watching her strut down the catwalk at the university's *Don't Walk* charity fashion show.

In their second year, Kate and William moved into a shared flat in Hope Street, where their romance blossomed away from the attention of the world's press and the rest of the students!

Eventually, in April 2004, William and Kate went public on a skiing holiday with friends. The couple were on the front page of every newspaper the next day, as people wondered if Kate was 'the one'.

After university, William went to train at Sandhurst and Kate started work as a fashion buyer at the clothing company, Jigsaw. It seemed the couple were drifting apart and in 2007 they did split up briefly. But three months later, Kate was back on the scene and soon their romance was back on track.

Did you know?

When they graduated from St Andrews on the 23rd June 2005, the vice-chancellor said to his students, "You will have made lifelong friends. You may have met your husband or wife," and he was right. One of the couples would go on to have a rather special wedding, watched by 2 billion people around the world!

Once they were back together, William and Kate are said to have made a pact that they were going to marry, but first William wanted to join the RAF and train to be a search-and-rescue helicopter pilot.

In October 2010, after his training had finished, the couple celebrated with a trip to a wooden lodge on the slopes of Mount Kenya. It was there that William proposed.

Their engagement was announced to the world on 16th November 2010. Kate looked stunning in a blue dress that toned beautifully with the £32 million engagement ring given to her by William. William said that the ring, which had belonged to Diana, was his way of including his mother on their special day.

When the wedding date of 29th April 2011 was announced, Britain was gripped by royal wedding fever on a scale that hadn't been seen since the wedding of William's parents thirty years before.

A Day to Remember

Once the engagement was made public, plans for the wedding of the year, if not the century, were underway. The next evening, Kate was seen slipping out of Westminster Abbey. The couple had decided that the wedding venue of William's grandparents and great-grandparents was the perfect place for them to marry.

William and Kate were determined to have the wedding they wanted. In typical, low-key style, Kate decided she wanted to travel to the Abbey by car, rather than in a glass coach.

Throughout the preparations, the main question was what would Kate's dress be like? Kate was so determined to keep her dress and the identity of the designer, Sarah Burton from McQueen, under wraps that she had top-secret meetings with her at Hampton Court Palace.

'Operation wedding dress' was so secret that even the lace-makers working on it didn't know who it was for until minutes before the ceremony, although it's fair to say that they had probably guessed the identity of the mystery bride!

Everyone agreed that it was worth the wait when they glimpsed Kate in an elegant ivory dress with a three-metre train and lace motifs representing the four countries of the United Kingdom. She also wore a tiara loaned to her by the Queen.

When William finally saw Kate at the altar, he was blown away by her outfit and whispered, "You look beautiful!"

After the wedding ceremony, William and Kate, who were now the Duke and Duchess of Cambridge, made their way back to Buckingham Palace by horse and carriage, past the huge crowds that had gathered to cheer them on their way.

Like his parents before him, William stepped out onto the balcony with his new wife. The crowd went wild when they kissed although one of their bridesmaids,

Grace van Cutsem, was less enthusiastic about the noisy fly past by the RAF, covering her ears as they roared overhead!

Royal duties done, the bride and groom went into the palace to enjoy their wedding reception with 650 guests.

Afterwards they partied late into the night, with the throne room turned into a nightclub, where William and Kate's first dance was to Elton John's *Your Song*.

Did you know?

After their wedding reception, the Duke and Duchess went back to Clarence House to get ready for their evening party. William drove them very slowly down the Mall in his father's classic Aston Martin – not because they were waving to the crowds, but because he had left the handbrake on!

The day after the wedding, everyone assumed that the royal couple would, like most newly-weds, jet off somewhere exotic on honeymoon.

The world was surprised when the casually dressed couple hopped into a helicopter and whizzed off from Buckingham Palace to a secret location for the weekend, then went quietly back to Wales for ten days.

One of the reasons was that William had to return to work as a search-and-rescue pilot. Another was that it allowed time for the fuss to die down as they hoped they could enjoy their honeymoon in privacy.

On the 9th May, Kate and William flew out to North Island in the Seychelles, where they spent time together at a plush villa, complete with swimming pool and private yacht. They also explored the island on mountain bikes, taking in the beautiful, exotic scenery.

After the amazing scenes all over Britain celebrating their wedding, and the excitement of their honeymoon together, the royal couple based themselves in Anglesey. William carried on working as a search-and-rescue pilot. It was a special time for the newly-weds, who enjoyed the privacy of their country cottage, where they could escape the world's attention and experience a little normality.

But they still carried out many public engagements and royal duties. Just weeks after the wedding, the Duke and Duchess welcomed the President of the United States, Barack Obama and the First Lady, Michelle Obama to Buckingham Palace. Kate wowed in a low-key but elegant high street dress which sold out within moments of the first photos appearing online, as people copied her look.

Kate also sparkled in an elegant full-length dress during their first public

engagement at a charity gala dinner at Kensington Palace.

Later that year, the royal couple took their first official tour abroad in July 2011, to Canada and the United States.

There were also a lot of smaller local engagements, supporting many of the charities that the couple represent. In no time at all, it was the Duke and Duchess's first wedding anniversary, just *one* of many royal celebrations in 2012!

What's Your Royal Profile?

Which royal are you most like? Kate, William, Charles, or Harry? Grab a pen and a piece of paper to note down your answers and find out!

1. Your ideal weekend activity would be:
a) Helping people in a spot of bother
b) A long walk on a windswept moor
c) Going to a party with your mates
d) Walking your dog on the beach

2. You book a holiday and choose:
a) An African safari
b) The wilds of the Scottish highlands
c) Skiing in an exclusive Swiss resort
d) A tropical island hideaway

3. You inherit some money and decide to give some to a charity that helps with:
a) Homelessness
b) Environmental issues
c) The armed forces
d) Anti-bullying

4. You decide to get a pet. You choose:
a) A black Labrador
b) A Jack Russell terrier
c) A polo pony
d) A springer spaniel

5. Your ideal way to get around would be:
a) A helicopter – with you flying it!
b) A classic Austin Martin car
c) A Harley-Davidson motorbike
d) A nippy VW Golf

An Incredible Year

Like every married couple as soon as the ink was dry on their marriage certificate, people started hinting about babies. Except, for William and Kate, there weren't so much hints as the not-so-subtle newspaper headlines screaming, 'Is Kate expecting a baby yet?'

But having a baby in 2012 would have been a little awkward for Kate and William. It was a very special year for Britain, with the London Olympics and the Queen's Diamond Jubilee to celebrate – their country needed them!

In 2012, celebration was the buzz-word and it seemed as if the whole country was decked out in Union flags and bunting.

First, there was the pomp and ceremony of the Queen's Diamond Jubilee, as the nation celebrated her 60th year on the throne. This was extra-special, as Her Majesty is only the second monarch to reign for so long, apart from her great-great grandmother, Queen Victoria, who ruled for 63 years.

Then there were the Olympics, held in London for the first time since 1948, and William and Kate played a central part, supporting the Queen and Prince Philip.

It was a great year for both the royal family and Britain alike and no one wanted it to end. As everyone waved their flags and watched athletes in the summer sunshine, little did they know that at the end of such a wonderful year, the Duke and Duchess would have more good news!

The Queen's Diamond Jubilee saw the royal family coming together for an incredible river pageant. It was the first time in more than 300 years that an event like it had been held on the River Thames.

The Queen and Prince Philip were joined by Prince Charles, Camilla, William and Kate, on a spectacular trip by royal barge, with more than 1,000 boats following.

Even the rain didn't keep people away, and at times the royal family seemed

amazed to see how many people had turned out to cheer them.

In the evening, the celebrations had a thoroughly modern twist, with a pop concert in front of Buckingham Palace. Crowds waving Union flags packed the Mall leading from the Palace to listen to world-famous pop stars performing. William and Kate were obviously enjoying themselves. But the loud music was a little much for the Queen, who wore earplugs throughout!

The success of the Queen's Diamond Jubilee celebrations made everyone proud to be British. But there was more to come in 2012, as the Olympics opened on 27th July 2012 with a ceremony created by the film director Danny Boyle. One of the highlights of the evening was a James Bond spoof, which ended with the Queen appearing to parachute into the Olympic stadium, which goes to show, it's not just the younger royals who are good sports!

William and Kate threw themselves into the Olympics as ambassadors for Team GB, alongside Prince Harry. They were seen at many events and, although they were there to represent the Queen, the sports-mad couple were genuinely interested in many of the events and were just as wrapped up in the excitement as the other spectators. Their love was once again plain to see as they hugged each other when British cyclist, Sir Chris Hoy, won gold.

Taking The World By Storm

It's not just in Britain that William and Kate have wowed the public. In 2011, they carried out their first overseas trip as husband and wife.

Kicking off the tour in Ottawa, Canada in June 2011, William and Kate were greeted by thousands of people. Many of them were so keen to see the royal couple that they had driven for hours to be there!

Some may have found the cheering crowds daunting, but as usual, William and Kate were relaxed and happy carrying out their royal duties. Kate is a natural with the public and by the end of day one, she had the Canadian seal of approval.

The successful trip finished in the United States, where they dazzled Hollywood stars at a gala dinner.

William and Kate's next tour was for part of the Diamond Jubilee in 2012. They went east to Malaysia then to Singapore. It was here, when they toasted with water instead of champagne, that the rumours began. Was a royal baby on the way?

Did you know?

In the past 61 years, Queen Elizabeth II has travelled to 116 countries on 261 tours. This makes her the world's most travelled head of state, but she has no souvenir stamps in her passport, because she doesn't need one to travel!

After Singapore, William and Kate's Diamond Jubilee tour continued as they visited Malaysia and the Solomon Islands.

A highlight of the tour was a visit to the Danum Valley research centre in Borneo. There they donned safety gear and were winched more than 40 metres up into the rainforest canopy, showing that the couple hadn't lost any of their love of adventure!

Probably the most enjoyable part of the tour was their last destination, the tiny and remote Pacific island of Tuvulu, where they happily joined in with the traditional welcome, wearing garlands and flower crowns. At the informal state dinner, Kate even popped on a grass skirt, and the royal couple danced the hula, to the delight of the islanders.

Their ten-day Diamond Jubilee tour complete, and with more nations wowed, it was time for the royal couple to head back to Britain.

They had come to the end of an incredible year, but William and Kate still had a dramatic surprise in store to round off 2012.

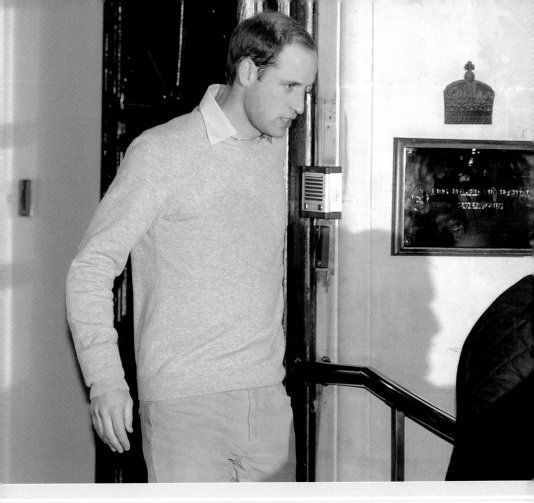

At the beginning of December, Kate was staying with her parents for the weekend, when she was rushed to King Edward VII hospital in London.

Reporters and photographers gathered at the entrance to snap William as he arrived to visit his wife. Then came the surprise announcement…

On December 3rd 2012, the Duke and Duchess of Cambridge announced that Kate was expecting their first baby.

The couple would probably have liked to have waited longer to announce their news, but Kate was suffering from terrible morning sickness and needed to stay in hospital for a few days to recover. There was little hope of them keeping it secret and so the decision was made to go public a little earlier than usual.

Everyone was overjoyed for the couple, but also concerned for Kate. As the story spread, rumours started that her extreme morning sickness was due to her expecting a girl or even twins!

After three days in hospital Kate was allowed home. As she left the hospital, Kate and William's delight at their news was obvious. But they remained tight-lipped about the baby's gender and due date. And so the guessing game continued.

At the age of seven, Prince William had told his mother he wanted to be a policeman so he could take care of her. But Prince Harry soon set him straight, saying, "Oh no, you can't – you've got to be king!"

The birth of the royal baby will make history now that the first-born child will be heir, whether it is a girl or a boy. Male or female, the royal baby will learn from an early age that much is expected of them as third in line to the throne after Prince Charles and William.

As Willliam once said about being king: "It's something I was born into and it's my duty," and a big duty it is. British monarchs rule over 16 countries, as well as heading up the Church of England and being on hand to advise Prime Ministers. As a child this must have seemed rather daunting to William – no wonder he thought he'd rather be a policeman instead!

Did you know?

Queen Elizabeth II wasn't born to be queen. Her uncle, Edward VII, was king briefly, but gave up the crown. So Elizabeth's father, Albert became king and was crowned George VI in 1937. Suddenly Elizabeth, pictured above with her younger sister Margaret, was next in line to the throne.

Prince Philip Mountbatten		
	married 1947	Prince Charles Philip Arthur George Windsor
Queen Elizabeth II		

Edward John 8th Earl Spencer		
	married 1954	Lady Diana Frances Spencer
Honourable Frances Ruth Bourke Roche		

Peter Francis Middleton		
	married 1946	Michael Francis Middleton
Valerie Glassborrow		

Ronald John James Goldsmith		
	married 1953	Carole Elizabeth Goldsmith
Dorothy Harrison		

Family Tree

married 1981 — | **Prince William Arthur Philip Louis Windsor** |

married 2011 — | **His Royal Highness Prince George Alexander Louis of Cambridge** born 22nd July 2013 |

married 1980 — | **Catherine Elizabeth Middleton** |

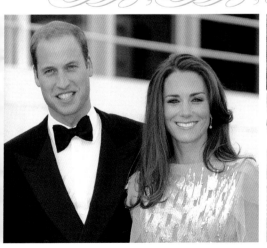
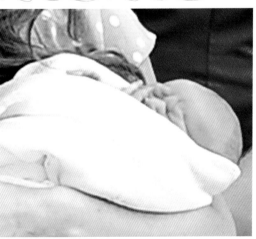

Even with all their responsibilities, there is still the chance for royals to have fun. The younger generation of royals have introduced a more relaxed, informal style that has impressed whoever they meet.

William is often described as being very 'down-to-earth' while Kate is fast becoming known for her natural, easy-going approach to people. Her fondness for high-street labels has also pleased fans, who can copy her look without spending a small fortune. Kate even pitches in to help out with the local Scout group in Anglesey, Wales, in her spare time.

The royal couple are just as happy to take part when they are doing their royal duties. On their trip to Canada in 2011, they even competed against each other in a dragon-boat race on Dalvay Lake, finishing with an affectionate hug when it was over. It seems that in William and Kate's hands, being royal is officially cool!

Waiting for Baby

Since December 2012, everyone has watched Kate's growing bump with eager anticipation. Every public engagement has made people pay extra attention in case the royal couple let slip any top-secret details about the baby ahead of time.

When Kate was on a visit to Grimsby, she was handed a teddy bear and someone in the crowd mistakenly claimed she'd said, 'Thank you I'll take that for my d—' before breaking off. In moments, the internet was buzzing with excitement, assuming Kate was having a girl.

The frenzy of speculation over whether the baby would be a boy or a girl continued throughout Kate's pregnancy. Every time Kate made a purchase or carried out a royal engagement, each gesture or comment was studied closely.

Then rumours flew around that other young royals had been heard saying the baby was a boy. When Kate was speaking to some army wives in Aldershot about prams she mentioned that she had bought a trendy Bugaboo in pale blue. This seemed to confirm things further. Suddenly, after months of people feeling sure the baby would be a girl, everyone wondered if it might be a royal boy after all!

It seemed that everyone would just have to wait and see as the royal couple and the palace remained tight-lipped about whether the baby would be a bouncing boy or a gorgeous girl!

The royal couple have also kept quiet on names, although they have hinted they have a shortlist. People felt certain that Alexandra and Elizabeth would be hot favourites for a girl and George top of the list for a boy. But that didn't stop Prince Harry winding the couple up with some rather unusual suggestions!

Although Kate had to take it easy at the start of her pregnancy, she soon bloomed and looked every inch the radiant mum-to-be. When their close friend William van Cutsem married at the end of May, Kate wasn't slowed down by her baby bump and it is said she spent the night 'rocking the dance floor' with William.

In between her royal duties and down-time, Kate was seen out shopping for her little arrival with the help of her mother, Carole. Then it was just a case of waiting for the big day to arrive...

Did you know?

When Prince William was born, an announcement was put up at Buckingham Palace, which simply said:

"Her Royal Highness the Princess of Wales was safely delivered of a son at 9.03 pm today. Her Royal Highness and her child are both doing well."

Test Your
Royal Knowledge

Does your royal knowledge rock or not? Find out with this super-speedy quiz:

1. Which university did William attend?
a) Edinburgh
b) Oxford
c) St Andrews

2. Where did Kate and her family move to when she was two years old?
a) Amman, Jordan
b) Abu Dhabi, United Arab Emirates
c) Anchorage, Alaska

3. What is Kate's brother's name?
a) Jason
b) Jonathan
c) James

4. Where did William and Kate spend their honeymoon?
a) Tuvulu, the South Pacific
b) North Island, the Seychelles
c) Kenya

5. What is Kate's middle name?
a) Elizabeth
b) Louise
c) Victoria

6. What is William and Kate's title?
a) The Duke and Duchess of Cornwall
b) The Duke and Duchess of Cambridge
c) Prince William and Princess Catherine

7. In which year was the Queen's Diamond Jubilee?
a) 2011
b) 2012
c) 2013

8. What is the royal baby's full name?
a) George Louis Alexander
b) James Henry Charles
c) George Alexander Louis

The Big Arrival

All around the world people have waited eagerly for news of the royal baby's arrival. It is the latest instalment in a love story that has captivated people since William and Kate's early days together at university, through their engagement and their spectacular wedding day.

This was no ordinary birth – it was history in the making, with everyone keen to find out whether William's heir would be a future king or queen.

The press and some die-hard fans were camped outside the Lindo wing of

St Mary's Hospital from the start of July, ready to snap pictures of the parents and their bundle of joy, but they were in for a long wait. For days they sweated it out in the blazing sun of a summer heatwave, in what was dubbed the #greatkatewait on Twitter. Finally, just before 6.00 am on 22nd July, Kate and William arrived at the hospital, slipping in through a back entrance to avoid the press pack. The wait was almost over – but not quite...

At 4.24 pm the future king finally made his entrance into the world, weighing in at 8lbs 6oz (3.8 kg), but the crowds that had gathered outside would have to wait until almost 9 pm to hear the news, which was announced by press release and was soon trending on Twitter. The birth was also announced in the traditional way, on an easel at the gates of Buckingham Palace, to the joy of the crowd that had grown as the day wore on.

The following afternoon, Kate's parents were her first visitors, followed by Charles and Camilla. Excitement grew when Charles said the new family would be leaving soon – all eyes were on the same steps where Charles and Diana had presented William to the world 31 years ago. At last, the royal couple appeared. Kate, glamorous as ever in a simple blue dress with white polka dots, beamed as she held their son in a beautiful white shawl while William, looking every inch the proud father, watched over his new family as cameras flashed and pictures of the baby were beamed around the globe.

Then William took his new son in his arms and the couple approached the crowds, chatting briefly in their usual relaxed way, with William even admitting he had already changed his first nappy!

Afterwards, William drove his new family to Kensington Palace, before they set off for Bucklebury the following day – after a visit from the Queen, of course! The couple will be glad of the privacy as they enjoy every moment of their first weeks together as a family. One thing is sure: William and Kate will make great hands-on parents who will carve out plenty of family time as well as doing all their royal duties.

Kate, who is quiet and unflappable, will make a great mother and the strong relationship between her and William means they are sure to adapt to family life quite quickly, especially with the support of both their families.

It's a fairy tale come true for the ordinary girl who married her prince. But unlike stories, this isn't the end. It is just the beginning for William and Kate, as they start life as a family, with their precious son, His Royal Highness Prince George of Cambridge.

What's your royal profile, page 52

Add up your scores for each answer and use the total to find out which royal you are most like:

1. a = 4, b = 1, c = 2, d = 3   4. a = 4, b = 3, c = 2, d = 1
2. a = 2, b = 1, c = 3, d = 4   5. a = 4, b = 1, c = 2, d = 3
3. a = 4, b = 1, c = 2, d = 3

15+: Sensible and level-headed, you are most like our future king, William. Warm and kind-hearted, you always look after those around you!

11-15: You are quiet, loyal, and calm. Unflappable and discreet like Kate, you love spending quality time at home with family.

7-10: Wherever there's a party, you'll be at the centre of things. Just like Prince Harry, you love to make people laugh and when you are around, things are always fun!

6 or below: You're quiet and a deep-thinker, like Prince Charles. You have a creative side and love painting and story-telling and also care about green issues.

Test your Royal Knowledge, page 86

1) c, 2) a, 3) c, 4) b, 5) a, 6) b, 7) b, 8) c